Eyes

Injury, Illness and Health

Carol Ballard

Heinemann Library
Chicago, Illinois

Design: Jo Hinton-Malivoire and AMR
Illustrations: Art Construction

Originated by Blenheim Colour Ltd
Printed in China by Wing King Tong

07 06 05 04 03
10 9 8 7 6 5 4 3 2 1

Library of Congress Cataloging-in-Publication Data
Ballard, Carol.
    Eyes / Carol Ballard.
        v. cm. -- (Body focus)
    Includes bibliographical references and index.
    Contents: Development of sight -- Eye care -- Eye injuries -- Looking at eyes -- Corneal transplant -- Light and dark -- Tears -- Inside an eye -- How do we see? -- Short-sight -- Long-sight -- Accommodation -- Retina -- Color blindness -- Optical examinations -- Using two eyes -- Eye diseases -- Causes of blindness -- Living with blindness.
    ISBN: 1-40340-750-9 (HC), 1-40343-298-8 (Pbk.)
    1. Vision--Juvenile literature. 2. Vision disorders--Juvenile literature. [1. Eye. 2. Vision. 3. Senses and sensation.] I. Title. II.
Series.
    QP475.7 .B347 2003
    612.8'4--dc21

                            2002152972

Acknowledgments
The author and publishers are grateful to the following for permission to reproduce copyright material:
p.4 Corbis; p. 6 Bubbles/Moose Azim; p. 7 Getty Images/Gibson; pp. 8, 33 SPL; pp. 9, 27, 40 Getty Images; pp. 10, 37 Actionplus; p. 11 DK; p. 14 Trip/A. Tjagny-Rjadno; p. 16 (top) Trip/A. Gasson; pp. 16 (bottom), 25 SPL/Martin Dohrn; p. 19 Trip/H. Rogers; p. 21 SPL/Custom Medical Stock Photo; p. 29 John Walmsley; p. 34 SPL/Adam Hart-Davis; p. 35 SPL/CC Studio; p. 38 SPL/Sue Ford; p. 39 (top) SPL/Paul Parker; p. 39 (bottom) SPL/Argentum; p. 41 AKG London/Private Collection; p. 42 The Wellcome Photo Library; p. 43 Popperfoto/Reuters/Gary Hershom.

The computer-enhanced image of an eye on the cover is produced courtesy of Science Photo Library/ David Parker.

The publisher would like to thank David Wright and Kelley Staley for their assistance with the preparation of this book.

Every effort has been made to contact copyright holders of any material reproduced in this book. Any omissions will be rectified in subsequent printings if notice is given to the publisher.

Some words are shown in bold, **like this.** You can find out what they mean by looking in the glossary.

CONTENTS

WINDOWS TO THE WORLD

Your eyes are the most important tools you have for collecting information about the world around you. Without your sense of sight, ordinary living becomes much more difficult.

You have two eyes, situated at the front of the face, protected by the bones of the skull. The bony hollow in which the eye sits is called the orbit, or socket. Above, the hairy eyebrows help prevent dust and dirt from entering the eye. The rows of eyelashes also help keep dust and dirt out of the eye, and the eyelids regularly sweep across the surface of the eye. Tears are produced to keep the eyes moist and clean.

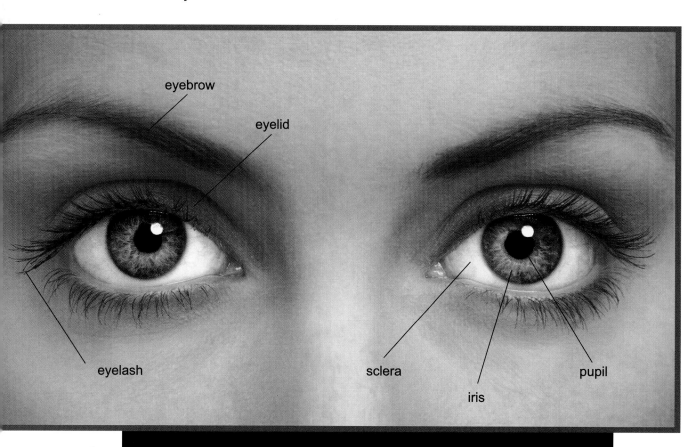

eyebrow

eyelid

eyelash   sclera   pupil

iris

Look at your eyes in a mirror. What do you see?

When you look at your eyes in a mirror, some features are very obvious. The white part of the eye is the **sclera**, and the colored ring is the **iris.** Right at the center is a black dot, the **pupil.** Although it may look solid, the pupil is actually a hole and is covered by a transparent layer, the **cornea.** Light enters the eye through the pupil.

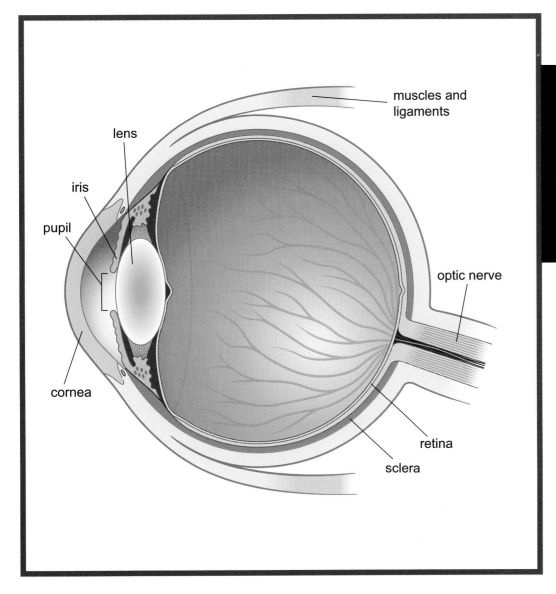

muscles and
ligaments

lens

iris

pupil

cornea

optic nerve

retina

sclera

The eye is held in place by delicate muscles and **ligaments.** These allow you to move your eyes. The muscles of the two eyes usually work together so that your eyes move together.

If you could look inside an eye, you would find that there are two large spaces, called chambers. The one at the front of the eye is filled with a watery liquid called the aqueous humor. Between the two chambers is a small disk of jelly, the **lens.** This bends the light as it enters the eye through the pupil. The larger chamber behind the lens is filled with a soft jelly called the vitreous humor. The curved inner surface of the eyeball is lined with a light-sensitive layer called the **retina.** The retina is linked to the **optic nerve,** which sends signals to the brain.

THE DEVELOPMENT OF SIGHT

When babies are born, they are able to see, but their vision is not fully developed. Their sense of sight, ability to focus, and ability to distinguish colors, shapes, and movements develop gradually during the first few months of life.

At birth

The structures of the eye are fully formed at birth, but the pathways of nerves that carry signals from the eye to the brain are undeveloped. Light enters the eye and the baby can see, but he or she cannot make sense of what he or she sees.

Newborn babies can detect bright colors and big patterns. They can focus on things 8 to 12 inches (20 to 30 centimeters) from their eyes. This is roughly the distance between the baby's face and the mother's face when the baby is feeding. Within a week of birth, most babies can see their mother's facial expressions.

The first month

During the first few weeks of life, babies are gradually able to distinguish between light and dark colors. They can distinguish between very different colors, such as yellow and blue, but cannot detect more subtle differences, such as different shades of green or pale pink and pale blue.

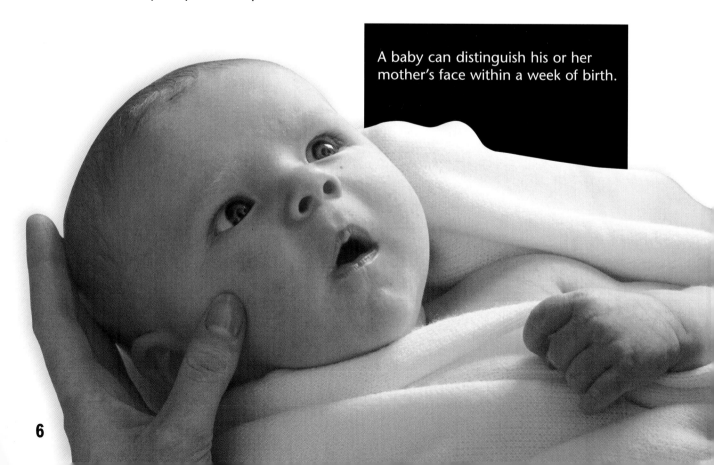

A baby can distinguish his or her mother's face within a week of birth.

Three months

By this time, most babies have learned to focus on things around them and to use both eyes to follow something that is moving. They blink if something is pushed toward their face. Their color awareness has increased, and they are beginning to develop their hand-eye coordination. If they see something that attracts them, they are able to reach out and touch it.

Six months

Most babies are beginning to see as an adult does by the time they are six months old. They can spot small objects and can accurately track movements up and down, backward and forward, and side to side. Their color vision is fully developed, and they are getting better at judging distances. Although they can see things that are near to them more clearly than things in the distance, they are also able to locate and distinguish things at the far side of a room.

This one-year-old can follow objects moving away from him.

One year

In most children, the sense of sight is fully developed before their first birthday. They can focus near and far, judge distances, distinguish colors, and track movements.

Eye problems

Within 22 days of conception, two shallow dips develop in the **embryo.** As the pregnancy progresses, the eyes form at the site of these dips. The process of eye development is controlled by a series of **genes.** If any of these genes are abnormal, the eyes may not develop properly. Other problems may be caused by the mother being exposed to a **virus.** Some scientists think that chemicals, such as drugs and insecticides, environmental pollution, and **radiation** may all be linked to babies born with deformed eyes, very small eyes, or no eyes at all.

Eye checkups

It is important to check that a baby's sight is developing properly. The sooner a problem is detected, the sooner it can be corrected. The first checkup is usually at birth, with a follow-up at six months. The doctor needs to make sure that the two eyes are working together and that the baby is not nearsighted or farsighted. If necessary, glasses may be prescribed to help the baby see and to ensure that both eyes work properly.

EYE CARE

Your eyes are very important, and you should try to take great care of them. You can do this by wearing the correct eye protection, keeping your eyes clean, eating a healthy diet, and visiting an **ophthalmologist** regularly.

Protection

Eyes can be damaged in many ways. When you engage in any sport or activity that may lead to an eye injury, it is important to wear the correct eye protection.

- Bright sunshine can damage the **retina.** You should never look directly at the sun. It is a good idea to wear sunglasses on bright, sunny days.
- Snow reflects a lot of light, and the glare can be as damaging to the eyes as bright sunlight. Too much exposure to glare from the snow can lead to snow blindness, which is like sunburn of the eyes. Ski goggles should be regarded as an essential part of your ski equipment.
- If you play football or ice hockey, wear a helmet with a face guard to protect your whole face, including your eyes, from a direct blow. If you normally wear glasses and need them for your sport, try to make sure that you have plastic **lenses.** Elastic straps can be attached to go around the back of your head to keep the glasses from falling off as you move.
- Science laboratories and technology workshops can be dangerous places! Always wear safety goggles to prevent splashes of liquid or solid particles from getting into your eyes.
- Many jobs require safety goggles or other eye protection. Welders wear full visors to protect their eyes from flying sparks, and many factory workers wear some form of eye protection to avoid eye injuries.

These children wear safety goggles to prevent splashes of acid and other dangerous chemicals from getting into their eyes.

Clean eyes

Like any other part of your body, keeping your eyes clean reduces the likelihood of infection. Carefully wash away the sticky substance called sleep that builds up around your eyes overnight. If you wear eye makeup, always remove it daily. If you wear contact lenses, follow the instructions carefully. Wear them only for the prescribed time and use the correct washing solutions.

Food

The food you eat affects your eyes. For healthy eyes, you need to eat a balanced diet. Make sure you include foods that are rich in vitamin A, such as carrots, eggs, fruit, leafy vegetables, liver, and dairy products. These are important for the eyes. The old saying that carrots help you see in the dark is true!

It is important to clean contact lenses very carefully to avoid any dirt or microorganisms from getting into your eyes.

Computer monitors

Staring at a computer screen for long periods can make your eyes feel itchy and dry. Sometimes they may also feel hot and look red. This is usually because you don't blink often enough when using a computer. Try to take regular breaks. And give your eyes a rest every now and then by looking at something at the other side of the room for a few moments.

Eye tests

It makes good sense to visit an ophthalmologist for regular eye tests. Most of the time, you will probably be told that everything is fine. But if there is a problem, it's best to find out as early as possible.

If you already wear glasses or contact lenses, regular eye tests are even more important. Your eyes change with time, so your prescription may change and need to be updated.

EYE PROBLEMS AND INJURIES

Bloodshot eyes

The clear **membrane** that covers the white of the eye is usually colorless, and its tiny blood vessels are too fine to see. However, if the eye becomes infected or irritated, these tiny blood vessels may swell and can be seen as fine red threads. This is called having bloodshot eyes. The eyes usually return to normal slowly after the infection or irritation that caused the problem has gone.

Conjunctivitis

Conjunctivitis—often called pinkeye— is an inflammation of the **conjunctiva,** the outer layer of the eye. It may be due to an infection or irritation and can cause buildup of a sticky fluid, discomfort, and watery eyes. Although conjunctivitis usually arises in one eye, it often spreads to the other eye. The treatment depends on the cause of the inflammation.

Spots and floaters

It is quite common to see gray specks or threads that seem to be floating around in the eye. These are tiny pieces of debris that move slowly around in the jelly that fills the eye. These do not cause any harm, although in rare cases they may indicate damage to the **retina.**

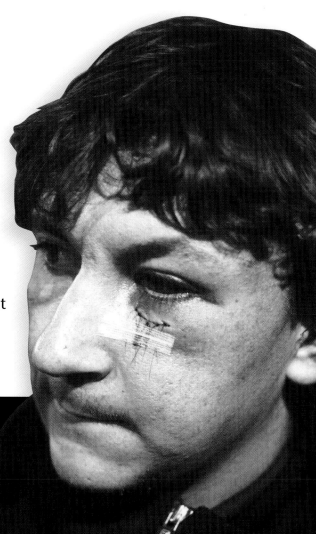

Scratched cornea

The surface of the **cornea** can be scratched by some accidental contact, such as a twig brushing against the face. The eye may feel sore and uncomfortable for a while, but this type of injury is rarely serious.

First aid for eyes

The main thing to remember about eye injuries is that you should let a doctor examine the injury as soon as possible. Stay calm and get expert advice!

This soccer player has suffered a blow to the face, resulting in a black eye. The bruising will fade, but a visit to the doctor is necessary to ensure that there is no injury to the eye.

Black eye

A black eye is not really an injury to the eye itself but to the parts of the face around it. If there is a strong blow to the face close to the eye, blood and body fluid may collect in the area, causing bruising and swelling. Treatment as soon as possible with an ice pack can reduce the swelling, and the bruising usually fades in a few days. It is a good idea to let a doctor check the injury immediately to make sure there is no damage to the eye itself.

Grit in the eye

If you feel a speck of something in your eye, your immediate reaction is probably to rub it. But don't! Instead, try blinking a few times. If the speck is still there, flush it out with a lot of clean, lukewarm water. If this does not work, you should see a doctor for help.

Cut eye or eyelid

Never treat a cut to the eye yourself. It needs immediate medical attention. Do not put pressure on the eye and do not rub it.

Flushing the eye with lukewarm water often helps remove grit or other particles.

Embedded object

If something pierces the eyeball, don't try to remove it! Cover both eyes to prevent them from moving, but do not put any pressure on the injured eye. If the object is small, the eyes can be covered with eye patches or sterile dressing. But if the object is large, you may need to use something such as a small cup. Get medical help as quickly as possible.

Chemical burns

If a chemical splashes into your eye, first check the label of the chemical to make sure that it can be mixed with water without causing a harmful reaction. If it can, hold the eye wide open and flood it with clean, lukewarm water for at least fifteen minutes. Then seek medical attention for futher help. Tell medical staff exactly what the chemical was, so they can decide on the best treatment.

LOOKING AT THE EYES

You are so used to seeing other people's eyes that you probably have not looked closely at your own for a while. Find a mirror and have a good, close look. . . .

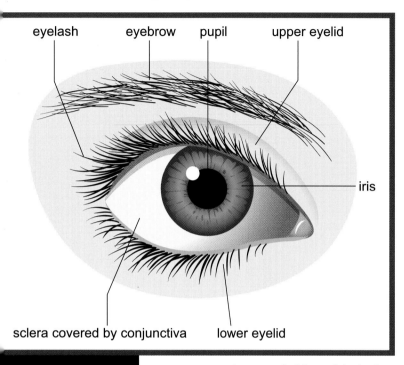

eyelash   eyebrow   pupil   upper eyelid

iris

sclera covered by conjunctiva   lower eyelid

Can you identify all these parts of your own eyes?

Eyebrows

Eyebrows are thickened ridges of skin covered with short hairs. They stick out over the bone of the skull above the eye, protecting the eye from dust and debris. They keep sweat from dripping down into the eye and act as mini sun visors, helping shade the eye just a little. They also act as shock absorbers, protecting the eye from blows to the head.

Eyelids

Eyelids are folds of skin that open at the front of the eyeball. They have four layers:

- an outer layer of skin with hairs called eyelashes
- a layer of muscle, which allows the eyelid to open and close
- a layer of fibers and oil glands
- a thin, see-through inner layer.

Eyelids protect the eye from dust and other foreign objects. As soon as something threatens the eye, a reflex reaction closes the eyelid. Eyelids also allow you to blink. As you blink, the eyelid spreads tears over the eyeball, keeping it moist.

Eye color

Eye color differs from person to person, and is determined by the amount of pigment, called **melanin,** present. Most dark-skinned people have a lot of melanin, so their eyes are dark. In pale-skinned people, eye color can vary from very pale gray to blue, green, and brown.

Iris color is controlled by a single pair of **genes.** You get one gene from your mother and one gene from your father. The gene for brown eyes, B, is dominant, and the gene for blue eyes, b, is recessive. This means that to have blue eyes you need two blue genes, bb. One brown gene and one blue gene, Bb, or two brown genes, BB, means you will have brown eyes.

Eyelashes

Eyelashes are hairs that grow along the edges of the eyelids. Each eye usually has about 200 eyelashes. Each one lasts about four months before it falls out and is replaced with a new one.

Sclera and cornea

Together, the **sclera** and **cornea** make up the outer layer of the eyeball. The sclera makes up about five-sixths of the layer, and the cornea is about one-sixth. The sclera is a tough, fibrous **membrane** and is the part usually called the white of the eye. It gives the eyeball its shape and protects the structures inside the eye. The cornea is see-through and lies in front of the **iris** and **pupil,** making a slight bulge at the front of the eye. It has no blood vessels, and it bends the light a little as it enters the eye. The **conjunctiva** is joined continuously with the sclera.

Conjunctiva

The conjunctiva is a thin, see-through membrane that forms the inner lining of the eyelids. It also covers the whole surface of the eyeball except the cornea. Because you need to move your eyeball, the conjunctiva is flexible around the edges.

Iris and pupil

At the center of the eye is a small black dot. This is actually a hole, called the pupil, through which light enters the eye.

Around the pupil is a colored ring. This is the iris. It controls the size of the pupil, by opening and closing.

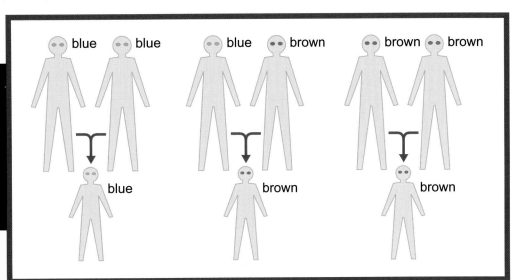

These diagrams show the eye colors of children from different parents.

CORNEAL TRANSPLANT

The **cornea** is the transparent, or see-through, outer layer of the eye that covers the **iris** and **pupil**. If a person's cornea becomes damaged or diseased, he or she will not be able to see as well as before the damage occurred. Corneal transplant now offers a way of restoring sight to people whose own corneas are damaged.

Corneal damage

Many things can lead to damage of the cornea, but some of the most common include

- a serious infection by **bacteria** or **viruses**
- a chemical injury
- a cut or scratch of the corneal surface
- aging.

Damage can affect the smooth surface of the cornea, its natural curve, or its transparency. Any of these may lead to poor sight and the need for a corneal transplant.

The history of corneal transplant

The first corneal transplant was performed in 1906. Since then advances in medicine have made it one of the most successful transplant operations. The cornea has no blood vessels, and therefore the white blood cells of the **immune system** cannot reach it. This is why the body is unlikely to reject the new tissue.

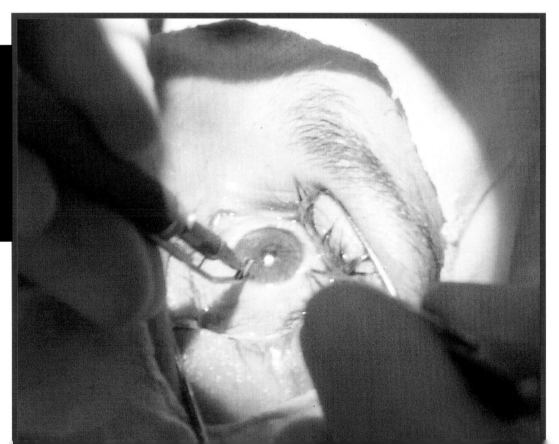

These doctors are performing eye surgery on a patient.

The operation

Although it has a very high success rate, corneal transplant surgery is very difficult. Surgeons work using a special operating microscope to magnify the eye 30 to 60 times.

The damaged cornea is cut with a circular blade that has a hole in the center. It is similar to punching out a circle of pastry with a pastry cutter. The damaged disk can then be lifted out.

The surgeon then cuts a disk from a healthy donated cornea and places it carefully into the hole. This new disk of tissue is held in place with stitches that hold it to the edges of the cornea.

The new cornea will allow the person to see clearly again within a couple of months of the operation. But the stitches must remain in place for up to a year.

After the operation

Although the patient needs to stay in the hospital only a short while, he or she must take great care. Special drops need to be put into the eye to help it heal and to ensure that it remains clean. Only gentle movements are allowed for a few days. This gives the new cornea time to settle into place. After a few weeks, the patient should be able to get back to normal, everyday activities.

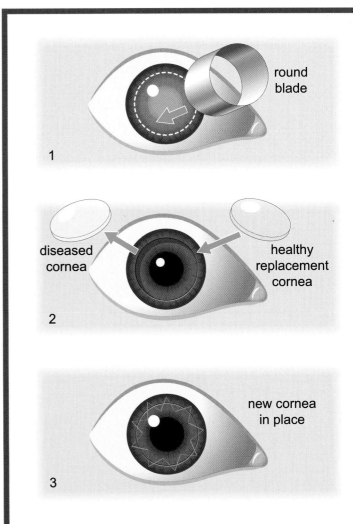

These diagrams show how a corneal transplant is carried out.
1. A disk of the cornea is removed.
2. A disk from the donor cornea is put into the hole.
3. The new cornea is stitched into place.

New corneas

After corneas are removed from a donor, they can be kept in an eye bank for up to a month. They are stored at 36 to 42.7°F (2 to 6°C) in a special solution that contains chemicals and drugs that keep the tissue as healthy as possible until the transplant operation. There are not enough corneas available for everybody who needs them, and waiting lists for transplants can be long. Scientists are trying to develop artificial corneas made from plastic to reduce this shortage.

Light has to enter the eye in order for you to see anything. Too much light can damage the eye, yet with too little light you cannot see clearly. The eye has its own built-in mechanism for regulating the amount of light that enters it.

The iris

The **iris** is a flat ring that hangs between the **cornea** and the **lens**. The outer edge of the ring is attached to folds of tissue called ciliary processes, which stick out from the ciliary muscles.

The iris is made up of two sets of muscle fibers:

- Radial muscles run from the outside edge of the iris toward the center, similar to the spokes on a bicycle wheel
- Circular muscles form the inner rim of the iris and are arranged in a series of rings.

These muscles contract in response to signals from the brain. They are antagonistic muscles. This means that when one contracts, the other relaxes. They are also involuntary muscles. You cannot make them contract by thinking about it. By controlling the size of the iris, these muscles also control the amount of light that enters the eye.

Muscle contractions

The radial and circular muscles have opposite effects. When the rings of circular muscles contract, they pull the radial muscles inward, shrinking the size of the **pupil.** When the straight radial muscles contract, they pull the circular muscles outward, enlarging the size of the pupil.

In normal light, there is a balance between the two, and the pupil is an in-between size.

In bright light, the circular muscles contract to reduce the pupil size and restrict the amount of light that enters the eye.

In dim light, the radial muscles contract, enlarging the pupil size to allow as much light as possible to enter the eye.

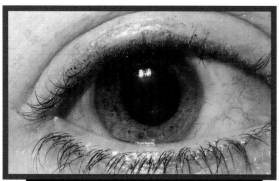

The top photograph was taken in dim light and the bottom in bright light. You can see how the size of the pupil responds to the different light conditions.

Check it out!

You can see these effects for yourself if you stand in front of a mirror in a bright room. Look carefully at your pupils, then shut your eyes and cover them without pressing on them. Open your eyes after a few seconds and stare into the mirror. You should be able to watch your large, dilated pupils shrink rapidly.

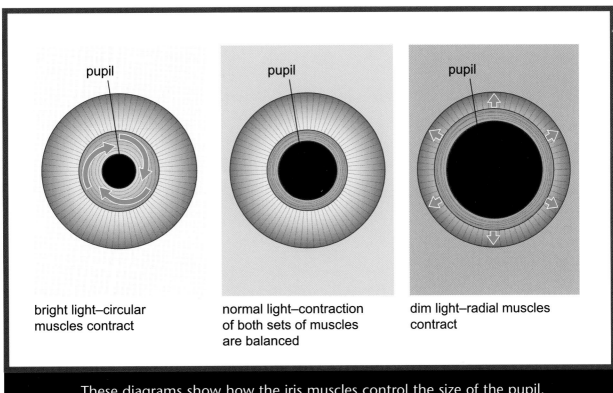

bright light–circular muscles contract

normal light–contraction of both sets of muscles are balanced

dim light–radial muscles contract

These diagrams show how the iris muscles control the size of the pupil.

Drug effects

If an **ophthalmologist** needs to see clearly into the eye, the normal opening of the pupil may not be large enough. He or she may put a few drops of a drug called atropine onto the lower eyelid. As you blink, the atropine is spread across the eyeball and acts on the muscles of the iris to make them enlarge the pupil completely. The effects of atropine wear off after a few hours, and the pupil size goes back to normal.

 # TEARS

Your eyes produce tears all the time, not just when you cry. Tears help keep your eyes moist and clean. Special glands under the eyelids produce the tears. They drain by way of the nasal cavity.

Tear production

Under each upper eyelid is a **lacrimal gland.** It is about the same size and shape as an almond. Each gland produces about .034 oz (1 ml) of lacrimal fluid, or tears, every day. There are between three and twelve lacrimal ducts, which carry the fluid away from the glands and empty it onto the inside surface of the upper eyelid.

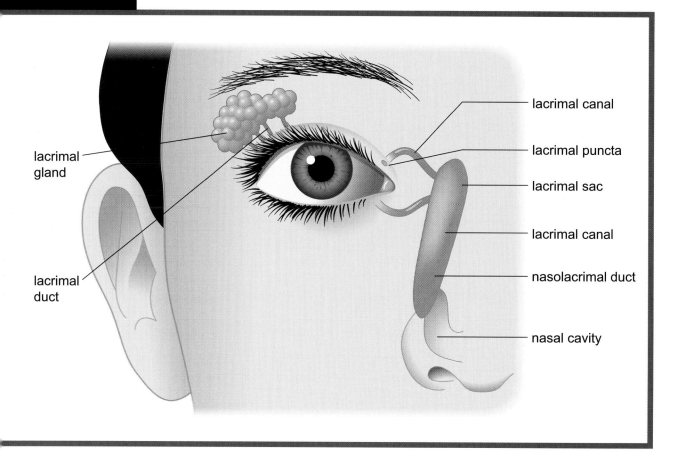

- lacrimal canal
- lacrimal puncta
- lacrimal sac
- lacrimal canal
- nasolacrimal duct
- nasal cavity
- lacrimal gland
- lacrimal duct

What do tears do?

Tears are a sterile, watery solution that contains salts, mucus, and an **enzyme** called lysozyme. They have four main functions:
- They wash dirt off the surface of the eyeball.
- They keep the surface of the eyeball clear and moist.
- They carry water and nutrients to the cornea and lens.
- They prevent infection. Lysozyme kills **bacteria,** preventing infection.

Blinking

You blink regularly, usually about once every 4 or 5 seconds, and each blink lasts less than 0.5 seconds. Blinking spreads lacrimal fluid across the surface of the eyeball and stimulates the lacrimal glands to produce more lacrimal fluid.

Where do tears go?

Once they have spread over the eyeball, tears drain into small openings called lacrimal puncta, which are at the inner edge of the eye. These drain into the lacrimal canals. From there the tears flow through the lacrimal sac and nasolacrimal duct into the nasal cavity. They leave the nasal cavity either by draining down the throat or into a tissue when you blow your nose.

The fumes from the cut onion have irritated this person's eyes, stimulating the production of excess tears.

Sometimes, you produce more tears than the drainage system can cope with. If you cry, or if your eyes are producing a lot of tears because of an irritation or allergy, the tears accumulate in the eyes and spill over. Tears also build up if the nose and nasal cavity are blocked. For example, if you have a bad cold, your eyes tend to be watery because the tears cannot drain properly.

Crying

The ability to express emotions —such as extreme happiness, extreme sadness, and pain or shock—by crying is thought to be unique to humans. No other animals are known to be able to do this.

Reflex tears

The eyes produce extra tears in response to emergencies. For example, tears are produced in response to fumes from an onion irritating the eye or the presence of a foreign object in the eye.

Why do your eyes sting at the swimming pool?

Many people find that when they go to a swimming pool, their eyes sting and start to tear. This is because the disinfectants used to keep the water clean contain a chemical called chlorine. It irritates the eyes, making them sting, and extra tears are produced to wash the chlorine away. You do not need to be in the water to be affected by chlorine. Some people's eyes produce extra tears in response to chlorine that has evaporated into the warm air around a pool.

INSIDE AN EYE

An adult eyeball is about 1 inch (2.5 centimeters) in diameter and has a complex internal structure. The outside layers enclose hollow spaces filled with liquid and gel. A system of muscles controls the shape of the **lens**. This focuses light rays onto the light-sensitive layer at the back of the eye.

This diagram shows the structures inside an eyeball.

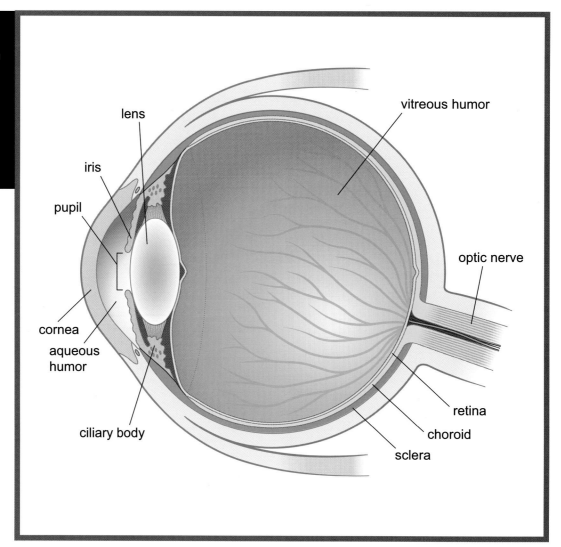

lens

iris

pupil

cornea

aqueous humor

ciliary body

vitreous humor

optic nerve

retina

choroid

sclera

Basic structure

The eyeball has three main layers:
- The **sclera** and **cornea** form the outer, protective layer.
- The middle layer is the choroid, which contains black pigment to prevent light from reflecting inside the eye. The choroid has a good blood supply, bringing nutrients to the internal structures of the eye. At the front of the eye, the choroid forms the ciliary body and the **iris.**
- The inner layer is the **retina.** It contains light-sensitive cells and nerve cells.

There are two chambers inside the eyeball, one in front of the lens and one behind it. The chamber in front of the lens is filled with a watery liquid called aqueous humor. It provides nutrients for the **cornea** and lens, which do not have their own blood supply. The chamber behind the lens is filled with a soft jelly called vitreous humor. The aqueous and vitreous humors press outward, helping maintain the eyeball's round shape and preventing it from collapsing inward.

Ciliary body

The ciliary body lies between the two chambers of the eyeball. It contains a ring of circular muscle, the **ligaments** of which hold the lens in place. By contracting and relaxing, the circular muscle controls the shape of the lens. The ciliary body produces aqueous humor and vitreous humor.

The lens

The lens is a see-through disk made of elastic gel. It bends light rays as they pass through it.

The retina

The retina is the light-sensitive inner layer that covers the back three-quarters of the eyeball. It sends electrical signals to nerves when it is stimulated by light rays. The retina contains a network of **capillaries,** which an **ophthalmologist** can see when examining the eye. The red eye effect that appears on some photographs is caused by the reflection of light by these capillaries.

The optic nerve

The electrical signals generated by light-sensitive cells in the retina pass to nerve cells and then to the **optic nerve.** The optic nerve carries the signals to the brain.

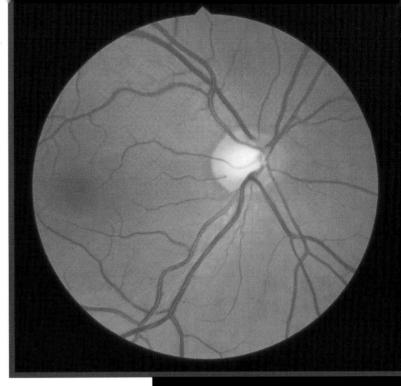

This photograph shows the retina as an ophthalmologist would see it using an ophthalmoscope. The fine red lines are capillaries.

Moving the eyeball

The eyeball is held in place by six muscles, each attached to the outside of the eyeball and the bones of the skull. They are some of the fastest and most precise muscles in the body, allowing the eyes to move up and down and from side to side. A squint or lazy eye may develop if the muscles of the two eyes are unbalanced or do not work together properly. This is usually noticed when a child is young and can often be corrected with eyeglasses.

HOW DO YOU SEE?

You see an object when light bounces off it and into your eyes. Electrical signals are sent from the eyes to the brain, which processes the signals so that you see the object. The process is similar to taking a photograph with a camera.

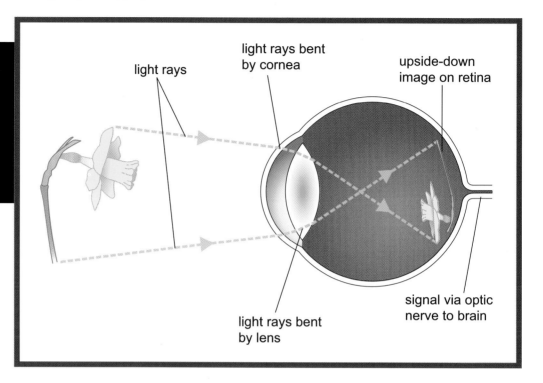

light rays bent by cornea

light rays

upside-down image on retina

light rays bent by lens

signal via optic nerve to brain

There are several stages in the process of sight, as light passes through different structures within the eye.

1. **Cornea.** Light rays travel in straight lines from the object to the eye. As they pass through the cornea, the light rays are bent, or **refracted.**
2. **Lens.** The light rays travel through the watery aqueous humor and the **pupil** to the lens. The lens bends the light rays even more as they pass through it.
3. **Retina.** The light rays travel through the gel-like vitreous humor to form an image on the retina. Light-sensitive cells called photoreceptors respond when light hits them. These cells send electrical signals to nerve cells.
4. **Optic nerve.** Electrical signals travel from the separate nerve cells to the brain by way of the optic nerve.
5. **Brain.** The signals from the optic nerve reach the vision center, a small area at the back of the brain. Information is passed from here to other areas, allowing you to associate what you see with what you already know. An example of this is the primary visual cortex, which may receive signals about a white triangle on a blue background, but your previous experience allows the brain to process this as a yacht sail on the sea.

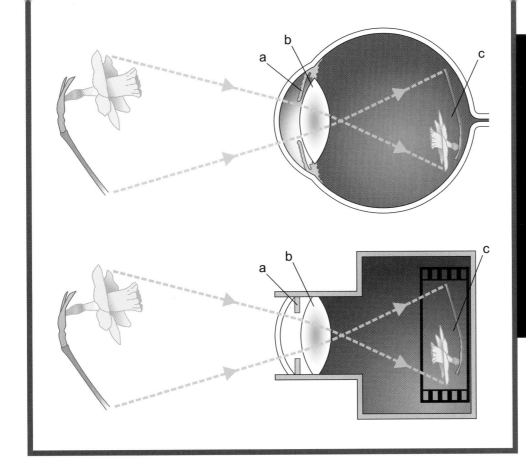

This shows how the eye works in a way similar to a camera:

a. aperture and iris control the amount of light entering
b. lenses bend light rays
c. images focused on film and retina.

Like a camera

The eye works in a way very similar to a camera:

	camera	*eye*
amount of light entering controlled by	aperture	**iris**
light rays bent by	lens	lens
image focused on	film	retina

Bending light

Light rays travel in straight lines and can travel more quickly through some materials than others. As light rays pass from air through the more dense cornea, they slow down and are bent. They are bent even more as they pass through the lens. This bending is called refraction. Both the cornea and lens make the light rays converge, or bend inward. They continue in straight lines through the vitreous humor, but then they cross over so that the image that forms on the retina is upside down.

Looking at refraction

If you put a straw in a glass of water and look at it carefully, you will see that the straw seems to bend where it enters the water. Look at it from the other side and it will seem to bend in the opposite direction. This is due to refraction. The light rays travel more quickly through air than through water, so the end of the straw seems to be in the wrong place.

NEARSIGHTEDNESS

The medical name for **nearsightedness** is myopia, and people who are nearsighted are called myopic. Although they may see things close to them very clearly, they have only a blurred view of things in the distance.

These diagrams show:
a. normal sight
b. light rays in a myopic eye
c. an eyeglass lens correcting nearsightedness.

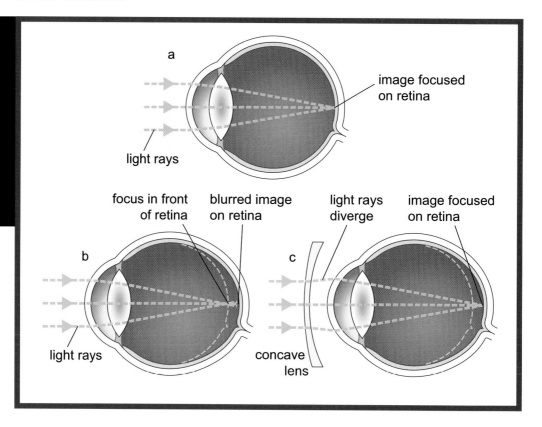

What causes nearsightedness?

There are two main reasons for nearsightedness:

- an eyeball that is too long
- a **lens** that is too thick.

The longer the eyeball or the thicker the lens, the more nearsighted the person will be.

Inside the eye

Light rays are bent by the **cornea** and the lens. These two structures should focus the rays so that an image forms on the **retina**. In a nearsighted person, the light rays focus in front of the retina. An out-of-focus image on the retina means that the person sees only a blurred image.

Nearsighted people may be able to see things close to them very clearly, but they have a blurred view of things farther away. The problem is worse when looking at objects in the distance because the light rays are more nearly parallel when they reach the eye. With closer objects, the light rays still **diverge**. People who are nearsighted usually need to wear eyeglasses or contact lenses for activities such as watching television, looking at a classroom chalkboard, and driving.

Correcting nearsightedness

Nearsightedness can be corrected with eyeglasses or contact lenses. The light rays are bent outward by a concave lens before they reach the eye, so the image is focused perfectly onto the retina by the eye itself. In physics, you may have learned that a lens of this shape will make light rays diverge, but this type of lens is not used to make glasses. Instead, a lens that is thinnest at the center and thicker toward the edges is used.

Treating nearsightedness
Laser treatment may be available for some nearsighted people. It involves using a laser beam to change the curve of the front of the cornea to make the image focus on the retina. Although this treatment has had some success, the changes are not reversible, and some people are concerned about taking any risk with their eyes.

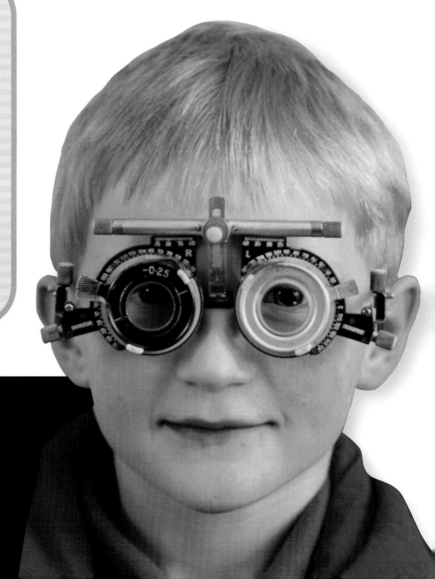

In an eye test, these special glasses help test how well a person can see the letters on an eye chart. A person with normal sight would see the letters clearly. To a nearsighted person, they would appear blurred.

FARSIGHTEDNESS

The medical name for **farsightedness** is hyperopia, and people who are farsighted are called hyperopic. This means that although they may see things very clearly in the distance, they have a blurred view of things close to them.

What causes farsightedness?

Farsightedness is the opposite of **nearsightedness**. The causes are opposite too:

- an eyeball that is too short
- a **lens** that is too thin.

The shorter the eyeball or the thinner the lens, the more farsighted the person will be.

Inside the eye

In a farsighted person, the light rays do not focus on the **retina**. The actual point of focus is farther away than the retina, so a blurred image forms on the retina.

The problem is worse with close objects, because the light rays are still **diverging** when they reach the eye. With more distant objects, the light rays are more nearly parallel.

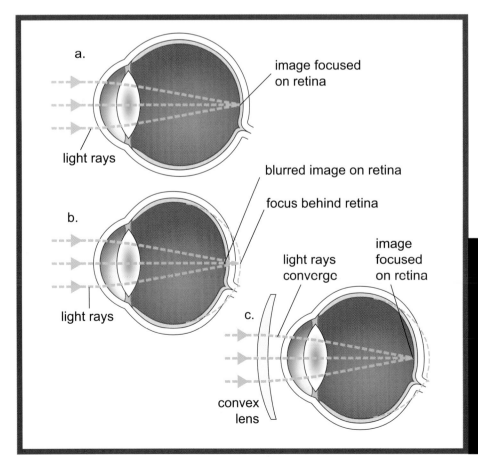

a.
image focused on retina
light rays

b.
blurred image on retina
focus behind retina
light rays
light rays converge
image focused on retina
c.
convex lens

These diagrams show:
a. normal sight
b. light rays in a farsighted eye
c. an eyeglass lens correcting the farsightedness.

People who are farsighted may be able to see things in the distance very clearly, but things closer to them are blurred. They normally need to wear eyeglasses or contact lenses for activities such as reading and writing.

Correcting farsightedness

Convex lenses are used to correct farsightedness. The lens is thickest at the center and becomes thinner toward the edges. The lens makes the light rays converge, so the image is focused onto the retina.

Astigmatism

Many people's eyes have an **astigmatism.** This means that the curve of the **cornea** or lens is uneven. Some parts of the image focus perfectly on the retina, but other parts of the image do not. This gives a blurred and distorted view of everything.

Astigmatism can usually be corrected with lenses that bend light more in one direction than in another. However, some astigmatisms are so severe that they cannot be fully corrected.

A person with normal sight can see his or her writing clearly.

NEAR AND FAR

You can see things that are close to you, such as this book. You can also look out of a window and see things in the distance. The adjustment that your eyes make to allow you to see things both near and far is called **accommodation.**

Focusing light rays

For a clear image, light rays must be focused. In a camera, light rays are focused by **lenses** to make an image on the film. The distance between the lens and the image is called the **focal length.** An ordinary camera has just one unchangeable lens. It will always focus light rays in the same way and so will always take the same kind of picture. Lenses are usually set to take clear pictures several feet away from the camera, and so objects much closer than that tend to be fuzzy and blurred. This is because light rays from distant objects travel almost parallel to each other and only need to be bent a little to focus them. Light rays from closer objects **diverge.** To be focused, they either need to be bent more or they need a greater focal length.

Professional photographers can change the lenses on their cameras to focus the light in different ways. This helps them to take pictures of both very close and very distant objects. To focus on closer objects, they use either a fatter lens that will bend light rays more or a lens with a longer focal length.

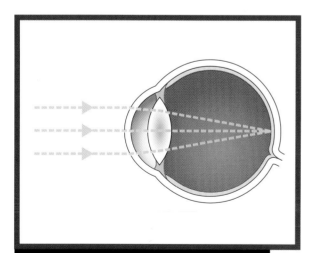

When you look at something in the distance, the light rays are nearly parallel. The lens is thin and flat because it does not need to bend the light rays much to focus them onto the retina.

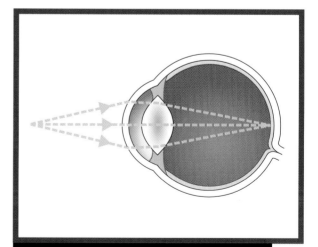

When you look at something close to your eyes, the light rays are diverging. The lens needs to be thicker and fatter to focus the light rays onto the retina.

In your eyes

You cannot change the focal length inside your eyes, nor can you swap a lens for a different one. Instead, some very precise adjustments take place inside your eyes.

The lens is held in place inside the eye by **ligaments** attached to ciliary muscles. When you look at things in the distance, the ciliary muscle relaxes and the suspensory ligaments pull on the lens, making it thin and flat. This reduces its bending power, so it brings the parallel light rays to a perfect focus on the **retina.**

An ordinary camera has a fixed lens. It can focus on things in the distance, as the light rays are nearly parallel. Objects closer to it will be fuzzy and blurred because it cannot focus the diverging light rays onto the film.

When you look at things closer to you, the ciliary muscle contracts, which makes the ligaments relax. As the lens becomes fatter and more convex, its bending power increases, and it is able to focus the diverging light rays perfectly on the retina.

If you look at objects at an in-between distance, the muscles and ligaments pull the lens to an in-between thickness, again focusing the light rays onto the retina.

How close can you see things?

The shortest distance from the eye at which an object can be seen clearly is called the near point. In healthy young adults, this distance is usually about 4 inches (10 centimeters).

Getting older

As people get older, their lenses becomes less elastic and the range of vision that they can accommodate decreases. This is called presbyopia. Older people find it harder and harder to read print at the same distance as they could when they were younger. By the age of 40, the near point may be 8 inches (20 centimeters), and it can increase to 32 inches (80 centimeters) by age 60. Many people overcome this problem by wearing reading glasses. Others choose to wear bifocals, which are eyeglasses that have lenses with separate areas for distance vision and reading.

THE RETINA

The **retina** is the light-sensitive layer that lines the inside of the eyeball. When light falls on the cells of the retina, they respond by sending electrical signals to **optic nerve** cells within the retina. These pass the signals on to the brain.

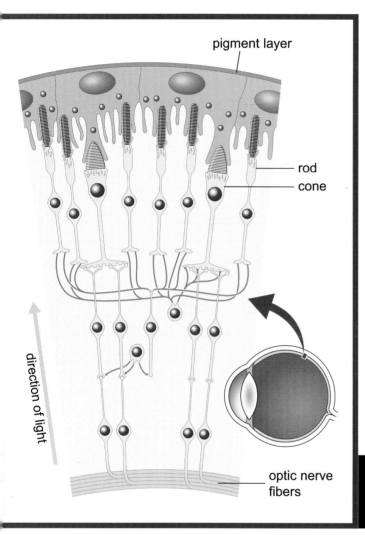

pigment layer

rod

cone

direction of light

optic nerve fibers

Cells of the retina

The retina is mainly made up of nerve cells and photoreceptors, or light-sensitive cells. At the back of the retina is a layer of cells that contain a black pigment. This layer absorbs light to keep reflections from bouncing around inside the eyeball. There are two types of photoreceptors:

- **Rods** allow you to see in dim light. They do not distinguish between different wavelengths of light. So when the light is dim, you see only shades of gray. Rods get their name from their long, thin shape. At the tip of each rod is a stack of about 2,000 disks that contain rhodopsin, a chemical that absorbs light. Each retina contains about 120 million rods.

This diagram shows the arrangement of the cells of the retina.

Color vision

There are three different types of cones, each containing a different light-absorbing chemical, or photopigment. One is sensitive to red light, one to green light, and the other to blue light. The brain distinguishes different colors by processing information about the relative numbers of each type of cone that have been stimulated. Looking at a red tomato stimulates mainly red cones, looking at green grass stimulates mainly green cones, and looking at a blue sky stimulates mainly blue cones. Light that contains a mixture of colors stimulates some of each type of cone. White light stimulates all three types equally.

- **Cones** can work only in brighter light. They distinguish between different wavelengths of light to allow you to see in color. Their name comes from that fact that they are shorter and fatter than rods and their tips are cone-shaped. At the tip of each cone is a folded coil that contains light-absorbing chemicals. Each retina contains about 6.5 million cones.

Parts of the retina

The exact center of the retina is called the **macula lutea.** It has a small dip in the center called the fovea, where only cones appear. This is the part of the retina where images are sharpest. When you move your eyes and head to see something clearly, you are trying to center the image on the fovea.

The point where the optic nerve leaves the retina is called the **blind spot.** There are no rods or cones there, so you cannot see an image that is focused onto it. You are not normally aware it is there, but you can prove it exists with this experiment. With your right eye closed, look at the web below. If you change the distance between the book and your eye, you will find a point at which the spider disappears. At that point, the image of the spider falls on the blind spot.

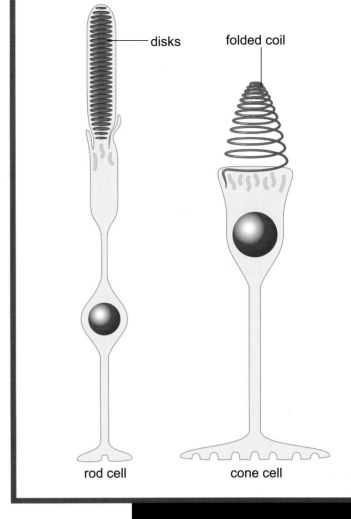

These diagrams show a rod cell and a cone cell. You can see the pile of disks at the tip of the rod and the folded coil at the tip of the cone.

Detached retina

Normally there is no space between the retina and the other layers of the eyeball. However, sometimes they may become separated, causing a detached retina. This is most common after a head injury or severe jolt, usually caused as the result of engaging in sports. The damage can often be repaired by laser treatment or surgery. People who have had a detached retina are often advised to avoid impact sports, such as jogging on hard surfaces and football, to prevent further damage.

COLOR BLINDNESS

Most people are able to detect differences between a whole range of colors. People who can detect no color, or a limited range of colors, are said to be **color-blind.**

Why are some people color-blind?

Color blindness usually occurs because one of the three **cones** of the eye is absent. The most common form of color blindness is red-green, or the inability to distinguish between red and green. This is caused by a deficiency in the red or the green cones. As a result, red and green are seen as the same color. If there are no red cones, red and green are both seen as green. If there are no green cones, red and green are both seen as red. Some people suffer from other forms of color blindness, such as blue-yellow, but this is much rarer.

An inherited condition

Red-green color blindness is an inherited condition, passed on from one generation to the next. Humans have 23 pairs of chromosomes, which contain all the genetic information. Males and females have 22 pairs of chromosomes that are the same, but the last pair are different. Females have two X chromosomes, and males have one X and one Y chromosome. The **gene** controlling red-green color blindness is only on the X chromosome. A gene for normal color vision always dominates the gene for color blindness.

These diagrams show how red-green color blindness is inherited.

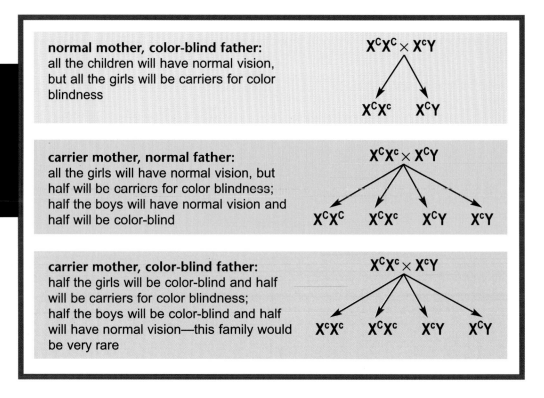

normal mother, color-blind father: all the children will have normal vision, but all the girls will be carriers for color blindness

$$X^C X^C \times X^c Y$$
$$X^C X^c \quad X^C Y$$

carrier mother, normal father: all the girls will have normal vision, but half will be carriers for color blindness; half the boys will have normal vision and half will be color-blind

$$X^C X^c \times X^C Y$$
$$X^C X^C \quad X^C X^c \quad X^C Y \quad X^c Y$$

carrier mother, color-blind father: half the girls will be color-blind and half will be carriers for color blindness; half the boys will be color-blind and half will have normal vision—this family would be very rare

$$X^C X^c \times X^c Y$$
$$X^c X^c \quad X^C X^c \quad X^c Y \quad X^C Y$$

male		female	
X^CY	normal vision	X^CX^C	normal vision
X^cY	color-blind	X^CX^c	normal vision, but Xc carrier
		X^cX^c	color-blind

Red-green color blindness affects 8 percent of men but only 0.4 percent of women. This is because people inherit only one chromosome from each parent. A girl has two X chromosomes, so to be color-blind she must inherit X^c from both her father and her mother. A boy has only one X chromosome, so to be color-blind, he needs to inherit only X^c from his mother. The table above shows the possibilities.

Testing for color blindness

People are usually tested for color blindness with Ishihara test cards. The cards are covered in patterns of dots of various shades. People with normal vision see numbers in the patterns of dots. People who are color-blind see only a random pattern of dots. They cannot distinguish between the colors.

Cards such as these may be used to test for color blindness. People with normal vision see the number or pattern, but people who are color-blind see only random dots.

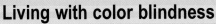

Living with color blindness

Being color-blind may give a slightly strange view of the world, but a person who is color-blind has never known anything else and so has nothing with which to compare it. There can be difficulties in everyday situations, however. For example, people who are red-green color-blind cannot tell the difference between red and green traffic lights. Instead, they have to rely on the position of the lights on the pole. They may also be unable to do some jobs where these colors need to be distinguished, for example, a train driver or a pilot.

EYE EXAMINATIONS

Even if you are not having any difficulties or problems with your eyes, it is important to have them examined regularly. Any problems that may be developing can be found very early. And the sooner they are detected, the sooner they can be treated! Eye exams can sometimes detect signs of disease elsewhere in the body, and your **ophthalmologist** can refer you to your family doctor, if necessary.

How often do you need an eye exam?

Some people need to visit an ophthalmologist more frequently than others. As soon as you were born, your eyes were probably examined by a doctor, followed by another checkup at about six months. Most preschool children have an eye checkup, and regular checkups follow every few years throughout a child's school years.

If you are having any problems—headaches, difficulty reading or seeing in the distance, blurred vision—see an ophthalmologist.

If you already wear eyeglasses or contact **lenses,** your ophthalmologist will tell you how often you need to have your prescription checked. Some people's sight stays stable for a long time, while others experience periods during which their vision changes rapidly.

What does an ophthalmologist do?

The ophthalmologist carries out several different tests. The exact tests depend on any problems you may be having. Some of the equipment may look complicated, but there is nothing to worry about. The tests do not hurt at all.

Distance vision can be checked by having you read a series of letters from a chart at some distance. Near vision can be checked by asking you to read different sizes of print held at arm's length.

A chart similar to this may be used to test how well you can see at a distance.

Looking at patterns on different backgrounds can help an ophthalmologist find out if you have an **astigmatism.**

The pressure inside each eyeball may be tested by directing a puff of air at the front of each eye. This may make you blink, but it does not hurt. High pressure in the eye may indicate glaucoma, a major cause of blindness. Its early detection is very important.

The ophthalmologist may want to see inside your eyes and will use a small flashlight to shine a tiny beam of bright light into your eyes. He or she may also use a larger piece of equipment that has a chin rest and frame to help keep your head still. For a more detailed examination, the ophthalmologist may put some drops into your eyes. The drops make your **pupils** dilate, which gives the doctor a clear view inside. Your vision may be blurry for a while afterward, but it will soon return to normal.

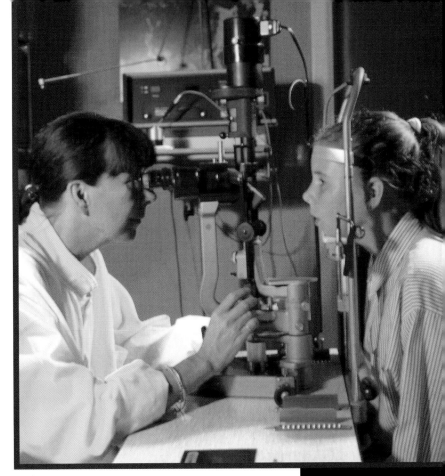

This eye doctor is examining the inside of a patient's eye to make sure everything is healthy.

Prescribing eyeglasses

Once the ophthalmologist has completed the tests, he or she may decide that your vision would be improved with eyeglasses. Using an adjustable frame, the doctor can try out different lenses, in slightly different positions, until he or she finds the prescription that is right for you.

Choosing and fitting eyeglasses

It is important that your eyeglasses fit properly and that the lenses line up with your eyes correctly. Today, there are many different styles of frames to choose from and many different kinds of lenses, too. You might prefer contact lenses instead, and again, there are many choices, so listen to the advice of your ophthalmologist.

Eyeglasses and sports
If you play sports, there are many special types of safety glasses and protective goggles that you can wear. Find out what is suitable for your sport, and make sure you wear them whenever you play.

USING BOTH EYES

You see the world around you in three dimensions. Things have height, width, and depth. You can also judge the distances between objects. This is possible only because each of your eyes has a slightly different view of things.

When you look at an object, you see the same object with both eyes. However, the left eye sees a view a little to the left of the view the right eye sees. Each eye sends a slightly different signal to the brain. When it puts the two sets of signals together, the brain is able to interpret the information, and you see a three-dimensional view.

When you look at an object close to you, each eye has to turn inward toward your nose. The brain receives signals from stretch-receptors in the eye muscles, giving it information about how much each eye has turned inward. The brain uses this information to figure out how far away the object is. The more the muscles are stretched, the more the eyes are turned inward, and so the closer the object must be.

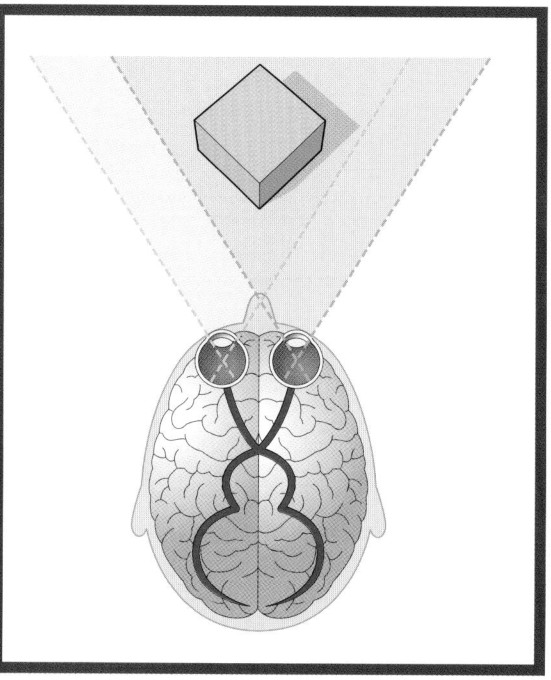

In this diagram, the blue triangle shows the area seen by the left eye and the pink triangle shows the area seen by the right eye. When the brain receives this information, it processes it and you see a balanced, three-dimensional view of the cube.

Different views

As the diagram shows, each eye sees a different area. The position of the eyes in the head affects how much these areas overlap and therefore affects the overall view. The eyes of animals that are likely to be the prey of other animals, such as rabbits, are at the sides of their heads. This gives them the widest possible view. Predators' eyes are at the front of their heads, limiting their sideways vision but increasing the accuracy of their forward vision.

Judging distance

Judging shape and distance is important in many aspects of your everyday life. For example, you need to be able to judge how far away from your feet a step is. And when you put out your hand, you expect to be able to pick up a drink without thinking about how far away the mug is.

Judging shape, space, and distance is vital for drivers and athletes, too. A tennis player, for example, needs to be able to pinpoint accurately the position of the ball, the racquet, and the lines on the court.

Peripheral vision

Usually, you look straight ahead and have a view of what is in front of you. Your eyes also collect information from each side. This is called peripheral vision. Good forward vision is essential in animals that hunt. This enables them to see their prey very clearly. Animals that are hunted usually have eyes at the side of their heads, giving them good all around vision for spotting predators. Humans have a field of vision of about 200 degrees—about 100 degrees on each side of the nose. You can test this by looking straight ahead, holding up one hand, and moving it backward slowly. Your hand will probably disappear from sight just before it is level with your ears. Detecting movement to each side helps keep you safe, especially when riding your bike or crossing a busy road. It is also important in some sports, alerting the player so that he or she can react rapidly. Some people suffer from a condition called tunnel vision, in which peripheral vision is extremely restricted. Their view of the world is simply like looking through a narrow tunnel. This can make some activities very difficult for them.

The brain uses the information from both eyes to enable this tennis player to judge distances accurately.

One eye

Some people can function extremely well with only one eye. They may have perfect color vision and be able to see outlines and details very clearly. However, they find it very difficult to judge three-dimensional shapes and distances, because their brain receives only one image and has nothing with which to compare it.

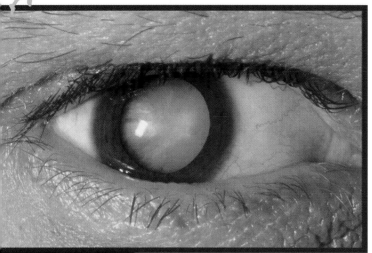

Cataracts make this person's eye look cloudy and white.

Cataracts

The formation of cataracts is one of the most common causes of blindness. The **lens** gradually changes from being clear and transparent to being cloudy and opaque. The quality of the person's vision slowly worsens until, eventually, he or she becomes completely blind.

Cataracts are usually thought to occur in elderly people, but they can develop in people with diabetes and other illnesses. Exposure to ultraviolet light, long-term use of some drugs, and smoking are also thought to be involved in the development of cataracts.

Changing eyeglasses prescriptions can help in the early stages, but as the lens becomes increasingly opaque, there will come a point where no further improvement can be made.

Glaucoma

Glaucoma mainly affects people over the age of 40 and is more common in women than in men. It tends to run in families, and scientists think that it may be passed on through the genes. Glaucoma occurs when the fluid inside the eye does not drain properly. As more fluid is made, the pressure inside the eye increases. At high pressure, the nerve cells of the retina may become damaged, and the person's vision deteriorates. In most people, the process is slow and painless.

Cataract surgery

Cataract surgery is routinely performed, often under **local anesthetic.** The patient is usually at the hospital for just the day, or perhaps overnight. The damaged lens is removed, and a new, plastic lens is inserted in its place. The patient's sight is fully restored within a few days. Eyeglasses may be needed to make minor adjustments, but the person's sight is often better than ever.

Trachoma

Trachoma is the single most common cause of blindness in the world. It affects more than 150 million people. A microorganism, *Chlamydia trachomatis,* infects the eye and causes conjunctivitis, which leads to the growth of extra tissue and blood vessels in the **cornea.** Slowly, the cornea becomes opaque and the patient loses vision. It is easily passed from one person to another and is also spread by flies. Trachoma is most common in countries with poor sanitation.

Although the **antibiotics** needed to treat trachoma are relatively inexpensive and available in much of the world, they are often very expensive and scarce among those people who are most at risk. By improving sanitation and water supplies, and by introducing drug distribution programs, the World Health Organization is attempting to eliminate trachoma completely by 2020.

Macular degeneration

The central area of the retina is called the **macula lutea.** As people age, it can slowly break down. This causes blurred and distorted vision and can eventually lead to complete blindness. The breakdown of the macula may be caused by blood leaking from **capillaries,** and laser treatment can often prevent further leakage, halting any further loss of vision. However, in some cases, the lining of the retina starts to break down. Until recently, this has been untreatable, but current research shows that some drugs may help. Tiny computer implants are also being developed to restore some vision.

Diabetic retinopathy

Some people who have had diabetes for many years may develop this condition, in which high blood sugar levels make blood vessels in the retina swell and leak blood. This can lead to blurred vision, **blind spots,** and floaters. As the disease advances, the retina becomes scarred, and vision decreases further. Regulating the blood sugar level and controlling blood pressure can help reduce the risk of developing diabetic retinopathy. Laser treatment may be used to seal blood vessels, and scientists are developing new drugs to help with blood vessel growth and repair.

This photomicrograph shows the retina of an eye in which macular degeneration is advanced. The second picture shows how vision is affected.

People may be blind for different reasons, but they all have the same problem—how to cope with everyday life without sight. Many things are available to help people who are blind, and modern technology is providing more all the time.

Why are people blind?

There are many different causes of blindness. Some people are blind at birth, perhaps because of a genetic defect or an infection during the mother's pregnancy. Some may have an illness or disease that slowly destroys their sight. Others may lose their sight suddenly due to an accident. Some drugs and chemicals can also lead to blindness.

Blindness may be due to damage to the eye itself, to the **optic nerves** that link the eyes and brain, or to the areas of the brain that are involved in receiving and interpreting signals from the eyes.

The Braille alphabet allows blind people to read and write.

Braille

In the early nineteenth century, a blind Frenchman named Louis Braille developed an alphabet of raised dots. For the first time, blind people could read by feeling the patterns of dots. They could also write by using a pointed tool to make their own patterns of dots on paper.

This system was called **Braille,** after its inventor. The first Braille book was published in 1827. Now the system has spread almost worldwide and has been adapted to virtually every language. Braille machines can be used to type Braille messages.

What can blind people see?

For some people who are blind, the world is completely black and dark. They cannot see any shape, movement, or light. Others have a small amount of vision, perhaps just a shadowy awareness of light and dark or the ability to detect some movements around them.

Blind or partially sighted?

A person with normal, healthy eyes is said to have 20/20 vision. This means that, at a distance of 20 feet (6 meters), he or she can read clearly what should normally be seen at that distance. If, for example, a **nearsighted** person has 20/40 vision, he or she can see at 20 feet (6 meters) what a person with normal vision would see at 40 feet (12 meters). In the United States, a legally blind person's vision has to be 20/200 or worse with glasses or contact lenses. A person with 20/200 vision sees from a distance of 20 feet (6 meters) what someone with normal vision sees from 200 feet (61 meters). The exact level of vision for a person to be classed as blind differs slightly from one country to next.

Communication

Most people read regularly for pleasure, for work, and for finding information and news. They read books, newspapers, magazines, computer screens, signs, and maps. They also write notes, checks, essays, letters, and e-mails. If you were blind, it would be difficult to receive and send information in any of these ways.

Louis Braille was born in 1809 and died in 1852.

Reading and writing are not the only problems that people who are blind face. They need to be able to live satisfying and independent lives and be safe at home and outside. Many things are available to help them achieve this. And many people who are blind are extremely successful in what they do.

Getting around

For many years, blind people relied on tapping a cane in front and to each side of themselves to help find their way along sidewalks. In the early twentieth century, the first guide dogs were trained to help people who are blind find their way around more easily and safely. Today, guide dogs provide invaluable help and support for many people who are blind. **Braille** and talking compasses can help with navigation. A special device can be worn around the neck that produces a tone or vibration when there is an obstruction ahead.

This woman relies on her guide dog to navigate her safely wherever she goes.

Helpful gadgets

Gadgets around the home make many tasks easier for people who are blind. Liquid level indicators fit over the edge of a cup and bleep when liquid touches them. This helps the person tell when the cup is full. Larger versions fit over a bathtub so the person knows when to turn off the water. Talking watches and clocks tell the time, and vibrating alarm watches provide a silent way of keeping track of time. Other talking devices, such as scales for food measurement and thermometers for temperature control, help with tasks most people do without thinking. Plastic covers for the ends of keys can have raised dots, similar to Braille, making it easier to find the right key.

Being blind should not mean that you cannot go out and enjoy yourself. Places such as concert halls often have seat numbers in Braille, which help people who are blind find the right seat. Theaters usually have audio facilities, so they can hear a description of what is happening on stage while they listen to the actors' voices.

Children who are blind

Until the mid-twentieth century, most people thought that blind children should be taught in special schools. But today, more than 60 percent of blind children in the United States go to regular schools. Some attend special classes for students who are blind or partially sighted, but others attend regular classes all day long with sighted students. Many blind students go on to college.

At one time, blind children were not expected to achieve much, if any, personal success. However, children who are blind have ambitions just like everybody else, and with the right help and support, they can achieve them. Perhaps the biggest handicap for people who are blind is not the blindness itself, but the negative attitudes of people around them.

Modern technology

Modern technology has provided some sophisticated equipment to help blind people. Closed circuit televisions (CCTV) make it possible for many partially sighted people to read. Simply put the book, birthday card, picture, medicine label, or whatever you want to read under a camera. An image is then sent to a television monitor and magnified many times. Some people link this system to a computer, which allows them to access the Internet.

Marla Runyan competed in the Olympic Games in Sydney, despite being blind.

Marla Runyan

U.S. runner Marla Runyan competed in the Olympic Games in Sydney in 2000. Any athlete who reaches Olympic standards must be considered highly successful, but the amazing thing about Runyan is that her eyesight began to deteriorate when she was nine, and she has only a very small amount of vision remaining. She can read things only by using a CCTV and computer. Instead of giving up, she has worked hard and achieved success in her sport. She even says that she does not consider her blindness to be a handicap when she is running because she can remember what running tracks look like!

This book has explained the different parts of human eyes, why they are important, and how they can be damaged by injury and illness. This page summarizes some of the problems that can affect young people's eyes. It also gives you information about how each problem is treated.

Many problems can be avoided or prevented by practicing good health behaviors. This is called prevention. Getting regular exercise and plenty of rest are important, as is eating a balanced diet. This table tells you some of the ways you can prevent injury and illness.

Remember, if you think something is wrong with your body, talk to a trained medical professional, such as a doctor or your school nurse. Regular medical checkups are an important part of maintaining a healthy body.

Illness or injury	Cause	Symptoms	Prevention	Treatment
astigmatism	uneven curve of **cornea** or **lens**	blurred and distorted vision	no proven method of prevention	corrective lenses may be used to reduce distortion and improve vision
conjunctivitis	infection or irritation, for example, from cigarette smoke	discomfort, watery eye, sticky fluid around eye	practice good standards of personal hygiene	depends on cause, but **antibiotics** may be used to treat infection
detached **retina**	often severe jolt or blow to the head	vision distorted by flashing lights and floaters, sometimes temporary blindness in affected eye	avoid situations where head may suffer blows or injury	surgical repair, often using laser
farsightedness	eyeball too long or lens too thin	blurred close-up vision	no proven method of prevention	corrective lenses may be prescribed to improve close-up vision

Illness or injury	Cause	Symptoms	Prevention	Treatment
nearsightedness	eyeball too short or lens too thick	blurred distance vision	no proven method of prevention	corrective lenses may be prescribed to improve distance vision
snow blindness	overexposure to UV **radiation** from the sun and reflected by snow	sensitivity to light, pain, headache, redness, and swelling of eye and area around eye, dizziness	for skiing or other winter sports, wear goggles or sunglasses that provide 100% UVA and UVB protection	cover eyes with cold compress, stay in darkened room, painkillers may be prescribed to reduce pain

FURTHER READING

Freedman, Russell. *Out of Darkness: The Story of Louis Braille.* Wilmington, Mass.: Houghton Mifflin, 1997.

Goode, Katherine. *Eyes.* Detroit, Mich.: Gale Group, 2000.

Pringle, Laurence. *Sight.* Tarrytown, N.Y.: Marshall Cavendish, 2000.

Stanley, Debbie. *Everything You Need to Know about Vision Disorders.* New York: Rosen, 2001.

Viegas, Jennifer. *The Eye: Learning How We See.* New York: Rosen, 2001.

 # GLOSSARY

accommodation changes that take place inside the eye to allow you to see close and distant objects clearly

antibiotic drug used to fight infections. Antibiotics destroy microorganisms such as bacteria or fungi, but are not effective against viruses

astigmatism uneven curve of the cornea or lens

bacteria group of microorganisms that can cause infection

blind spot point where the optic nerve leaves the retina

Braille alphabet of raised dots that allows people who are blind to read

capillary very fine blood vessel

color-blind not able to detect differences between colors

cone one of three sets of cells in the retina responsible for color vision

conjunctiva delicate outer layer of the eye

cornea see-through layer at the front of the eye

diverge when objects move away from each other

embryo earliest stage of development of a baby inside the mother's body

enzyme protein that helps chemical reactions take place

farsightedness condition in which a person can see distant things clearly, but close things appear blurred

focal length distance between a lens and the image

gene tiny part of a chromosome that controls one characteristic

immune system body's defense mechanisms against infection and disease

iris colored, muscular ring at the center of the eye

lacrimal gland place where tears are produced

lens jellylike disk that bends light that enters the eye, or any piece of see-through material that works in a way similar to the lens of the eye for focusing rays of light

ligament strong cord that binds body structures together

local anesthetic drug given to numb a part of the body

macula lutea sensitive central area of the retina

melanin pigment that gives the iris its color

membrane thin covering layer of tissue

nearsightedness condition in which a person can see close things clearly, but distant things appear blurred

ophthalmologist doctor who examines and treats eyes

optic nerve nerve that carries electrical signals from the retina to the brain

pupil hole at the front of the eye through which light enters the eye

radiation waves of energy that may be harmful

refraction bending of light as it passes through different materials

retina light-sensitive layer at the back of the eye

rod type of cell in the retina responsible for vision in dim light

sclera white surface layer of the eye

virus microbe that uses the body's own cells to make copies of itself

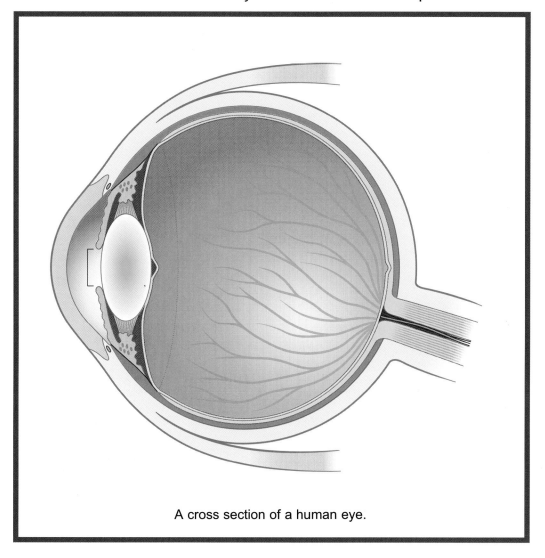

A cross section of a human eye.

INDEX